SIX WAYS TO CHECK
YOUR LEADINGS

Mark T. Barclay

First Printing 1997

ISBN 0-944802-18-4

Copyright © 1997 Mark T. Barclay, Author
Published by: Mark Barclay Ministries
aka Mark Barclay Publications
All Rights Reserved
Printed in USA

Write:
Mark Barclay Ministries
P.O. Box 588, Midland, MI 48640-0588

CONTENTS

A Word From the Author

Text

Introduction

Chapter 1 — Do You Have the Plan of God?
The *What* 1

Chapter 2 — Do You Know the Will of God?
The *How*. 5

Chapter 3 — Do You Know the Timing of God?
The *When*. 11

Chapter 4 — Do You War According to Prophecy? 15

Chapter 5 — Do You Seek Confirmations? 19

Chapter 6 — Do You Have Church Leadership
Approval?. 23

Prayer of Salvation

A WORD FROM THE AUTHOR

Before you read this book, please know that I am a born-again, water-baptized, Spirit-filled Christian. I believe in the supernatural leadership of Jesus Christ, the gifts and manifestations of the Holy Spirit, and the government of God in believers' lives. I am very aware of the spiritual world.

I want to help you be accurate and enjoy precision in your spiritual life. There is no good reason to be deceived, seduced, or led astry, not even in these last days.

On the following pages of this book, you are going to read some very blunt and bold things. I believe these things are very accurate and summarize the basic misconceptions, confusion, and fables of Christians today as well as Bible solutions to live a good, clean, stable life with Jesus.

I hope you'll enjoy this book and that it helps and challenges you to the maximum.

— Mark T. Barclay

TEXT

"Verily, verily, I say unto you, He that entereth not by the door into the sheepfold, but climbeth up some other way, the same is a thief and a robber.

But he that entereth in by the door is the shepherd of the sheep.

To him the porter openeth; and the sheep hear his voice; and he calleth his own sheep by name, and leadeth them out.

And when he putteth forth his own sheep, he goeth before them, and the sheep follow him: for they know his voice.

And a stranger will they not follow, but will flee from him: for they know not the voice of strangers."

John 10:1-5

"My son, keep thy father's commandment . . .

Bind them continually upon thine heart, and tie them about thy neck.

When thou goest, it shall lead thee; when thou sleepest, it shall keep thee; and when thou awakest, it shall talk with thee."

Proverbs 6:20-22

INTRODUCTION

FINDING YOUR COMPASS

Many people today are voicing how they are receiving direction and leadings in their life, and I notice these things always have God's name on them. People feel led to do this and led to do that. They say that God told them to do this or to do that, or that the Lord revealed this or revealed that. I hear these cliches quite often: The Lord said, the Lord showed me, the Lord revealed to me, and on and on and on.

Many of these people are not hearing from God at all. Many are being led astray. Many are following other voices. There are many voices in the world today—the voice of satan and demonic influences, the voice of the flesh and desires, the voice of your friends and family members, and more.

Jesus said about His sheep that they follow *His voice* and not the voice of strangers. (Read John 10:1-5.) We have been given an inner ear to hear the voice of our Savior and Lord, Jesus Christ of Nazareth. Yet Christians do some of the weirdest, goofiest things I have ever seen or heard. I mean some of them are first-class space cadets. When these spooky saints come to church, I'd like to ask them if the cloud or magic carpet that they rode in on is tied up outside.

Many people border on mysticism and a world of fantasy. GOD IS NOT A GOOFY GOD. He doesn't intend for His people to be goofy either. Some Christians see, feel, or discern demons in everything around them. They witness demons in their bread boxes, cupboards, and on and on. One person wanted me to cast a demon out of their home lighting system because this so-called demon was hindering the lights and causing them to dim and blink. Come to find out, the "demon" was their water pump turning on to build up pressure—it drew enough power to dim the lights.

Another person wanted to cast out of me the demon of postnasal drip. I could take these same "exorcists" to the mission field with me and show them demons that would *scare* the postnasal drip out of them. Most of these popular demon chasers have never tackled real demons, and if they ever did, it would be a "sons of Sceva" episode all over again.

It seems that staying in the main flow of Jesus is one of the most difficult things for believers to do, and I'm including some preachers. There are two categories of people who can, perhaps, be led astray more easily than others: intercessors and ministers. This is because both of these categories of people are so hungry for revelation, insight, and direction—they want to stay so close to the will of God, present the truths of God, and tell everyone they heard from God.

If we are not careful, we ministers and intercessors will come up with the most goofy, flaky, and spooky things that have ever hit Christianity. All this will be under the title of, "The Lord showed me . . ." It always gets me how one man will stand up and say, "The Lord showed me this," and then another man will stand up and say, "The Lord showed me that," and they are contrary to one another. No, God is not confused. "This" and "that" had better match if the Lord is "doing" and "showing." Amen? If they don't match, then somebody didn't hear too accurately from God.

My wife Vickie once did a teaching titled "Your Word Is Good Enough." In this she reminded us about *our* word. We don't always have to say, the Lord said, the Lord told me, the Lord led me, or the Lord showed me.

There are so many people who come up to me and say, "Oh Brother, I feel led of the Lord to give you some money." Well, I'll take it, and I'll thank you for it, but you know what would be just as good? If these people would just come up and say, "I love you, and I want to give you some money." You see, I already know that the Lord loves me, and I already know that He is generating funds to take care of me. I might need *your* love or *your* encouragement. I have had people come to me and say, "I am going to give this to you, Brother Barclay [sniff, sob, sob, weep]. The Lord told me to sacrifice this and give it to you [sniff, sniff, sob, sob, sob], and it means so much to me." I feel like telling them to keep it. They make me feel like I am robbing them—with God's permission. They are squalling and bawling and wiping their nose and then say "The Lord said . . ."

What happened to "we said" or "I said"? What happened to "I love you Brother, and I want to bless you" or "I want to give you something Sister, and I don't have to have the Lord motivate me to do it. I do it out of LOVE."? Amen!

The Bible says that we are to give according to what *we* purpose in our hearts. (Read 2 Corinthians 9:7.) I always tell people this: If you are waiting for God to tell you what to give in the offerings, you are insensitive, and you are not listening carefully enough to what is in your own heart. Any time the Lord has to supernaturally supercede your situation and place a command or demand upon you in order to get you to give money in the offering, it is because you were not going to do it of your own free will. When done of your own free will, it shows a desire to bless one of your brothers or sisters in the house of the Lord or bless the house of the Lord. Because you're not going to give of your own free will, the Lord Himself, through the communication systems of the Kingdom, has to stir your spirit man to cause you to give something in this offering. Then we stand up—unashamed—and say the Lord told me to give $20. Well, if He did, don't tell everybody, because you are just displaying how insensitive and stingy you were before the Lord commanded you to be a giver. We shouldn't need a command to be givers. We are supposed to purpose in our heart to meet every need that we see—to try to add something to every need that is around us.

There are so many sad stories to tell about people who are trying to follow God but are being so deceived. There are many cults and cultish leaders in the world today teaching unscriptural practices on how to be holy. You know, you've seen some of them. Also religion itself which is not always in line with God's Word will lead you into confusion, bondage, and darkness.

God's people know His voice and don't even pay attention to the voice of strangers. When a person begins to recognize the voice of Jesus, they know for a fact that all of these other things will never take the place of that powerful, yet gentle voice of the Savior. Jesus said that His sheep would never follow the voice of strangers. In fact, they would run away from a stranger because they do not recognize a stranger's voice. (Read John 10:5.)

Let me use a natural illustration here. In Marine Corps boot camp after about two weeks of recruit training, every platoon of young marines has a special knack of memorizing the voice of their platoon sergeant. They know the cadence he calls for them to march to. They know when he commands, "Lights out," or gives some other command, because they recognize his voice. They don't in the beginning, but after just a few days of hearing his commands night and day, they recognize his voice.

The Marine sergeants used to tease one another. They would stand in the mess hall doorway, and another man's platoon would be outside lined up and ready to march. They would yell a command to the other sergeant's platoon. If the recruits responded to the strange voice, it was bad for them. It was a mockery to a platoon sergeant when a different platoon sergeant could get recruits to obey his commands.

Recruits would get so finely tuned in communications that their sergeant could sit in the platoon hut (just before taps, just before lights out, they never had to see his face, he would never have to come out) and just speak the word only. They could hear voices go up and down the street in that recruit depot as the different Marine sergeants would yell out to *their* men, "Lights out." Then you would hear the platoon recruits yell back, "Sir, lights out, aye, aye, sir," and all the lights would go out in that block. This same command could be heard all up and down the road as other platoon sergeants were barking their orders, but somehow those recruits could pick out the voice of their leader. All the other sergeants could yell, but they knew when their platoon sergeant yelled a command because they could recognize his voice.

This is a very simple way to explain it, but this is the way it is with Christians following Jesus. You will hear a lot of voices in this world, a lot of voices giving commands, but I'm telling you there is something about the voice of the Lord Jesus Christ that ministers to the heart of a believer. If we are listening to that voice, we'll be sure to never follow the voice of a stranger. Many voices! Many voices! In this world, my friend, there are many voices, and most of them are voices that are strange to the Kingdom of God, and you have to be oh, so cautious and careful that you listen to the *voice of your Savior* and that you can recognize it. It doesn't always have to come in an earthquake or a fire—usually it is that soft, still voice on the inside of you. Sometimes it comes through church leadership, and sometimes it will come to you in the things you read in your Bible while praying.

Please study the remainder of this book carefully, and let it be a guide to help you follow Jesus, enjoying the comfort of a stable Christian life.

CHAPTER 1
DO YOU HAVE THE PLAN OF GOD?
THE *WHAT*

"Remember ye not the former things, neither consider the things of old.

Behold, I will do a new thing; now it shall spring forth; shall ye not know it? I will even make a way in the wilderness, and rivers in the desert."

Isaiah 43:18-19

Ask yourself this question: Do I have the plan of God for my life and ministry? Most people are going to answer no. The people who answer yes will probably only know a part of the plan.

We have to know the plan of God. Many people have a plan for their life and ministry, but it isn't God's plan. Only a few people have God's plan. It is the will of the Lord that all believers—not just a few—know the plan of God for their lives.

Some people think God is a joker, trickster, or magician. He is not! God will not trick you or deceive you just to see if you are listening or willing to do something. Many

1

people stick to the old fable: The Lord just wanted to test me to see whether or not I would do it. He really doesn't want me to do it; He was just testing me to see whether or not I would. How sad! Sometimes I wonder how people get such a low opinion of God.

Some people ask me, "Brother Barclay, what about Abraham? Didn't God test him to see if he would really kill his son on the altar?" If you'll recall, Abraham took everything to the altar that was needed to sacrifice and worship, except for God's portion. Number two, there was a sacrifice. Abraham did go through with it. God wasn't joking him or tricking him. Abraham *did not* bring the altar and wood back home with him. It was not a trick. God *did not* stop Abraham at the last minute and tell him to go home, that He was just testing him, kidding him, or practicing trickery. No! God provided a miracle supply to a very obedient and faithful man who *was going through with the plan.* Each day presents opportunities to *prove ourselves* to God. This is part of our servanthood, but God doesn't lead us through it with deception and trickery.

God was not teasing or pulling a joke on Noah when He commanded the ark to be built. God gives clear, precise directions. He didn't give Noah a plan to build an ark and then say when it was all built, "Ha, ha, I just wanted to see if you would do it." That is not God! God didn't give Moses the children of Israel, send them to the Red Sea, tell him to hold out his rod there for the Red Sea to split, to say, "Ha, ha, I just wanted to see if you would do it. Just checking out your faithfulness, Moses." Why would God do that? God knows your church attendance, and God knows your tithing record. God knows how you and your wife get along, and He doesn't have to pull tricks to find out.

Jehovah is giving clear, precise directions (for example, when He gave instructions for the tabernacle): "Use this color and this size" or "Build me an ark to the very cubit" or "Bring in your tithe exactly like this."

Please don't get caught up in the deception that you have to fleece God, try to fool God, or trick God. He doesn't play those kinds of games. Those are human games. They are psychological games. God doesn't play those games with your life. God is concerned with you. God loves you. God knows we are already dull of hearing, and He is not in the business of confusing us more. He is not the author of confusion by telling you to do something and then telling you it was just a joke or saying that He just wanted to see if we were faithful.

What did Isaiah reveal to us? God is doing a new thing, and we would know it. We would see it as plain as a river flowing through a desert. That's right! We would see it just as clear as a highway cut through a jungle wilderness.

DO YOU HAVE THE PLAN OF GOD FOR YOUR LIFE? Do you know *what* God wants you to do? Do you know *what* God wants you to be? Do you know *what* God wants you to say? The *WHAT* of God is the *PLAN* of God.

How do we find this plan (or *what*) for our lives? We pray and fellowship with the Lord. We read the Scriptures on a very continuous basis and see *what* God is saying to us. We listen to the anointed leadership of the church for guidance and supernatural vision. We fast and pray, according to Isaiah 58:8-12, and God promises to meet us there.

Listen, believer, there is no sense being concerned about the will of God or the timing of the Lord, prophecy, confirmation, or anything else if you have never consecrated yourself long enough to hear from God on the *whats*. Whys, whens, whos, etc., are all secondary to what God has for us—His plan.

You will know His plan. He will put it in you, and you will wrestle with it until you cannot get it out of you. It will just stick with you. The devil is so sporadic, he will tell you to do *this* today and *that* tomorrow, and why don't you start *this* and why don't you start *that*. You may start a hundred things and finish none. God will finish and complete the work that He has started in you, and He doesn't change His mind that often about you. If it is the plan of God, it will gnaw at you if you are being rebellious, and it will excite you if you are following after it.

CHAPTER 2
DO YOU KNOW THE WILL OF GOD?
THE *HOW*

"I beseech you therefore, brethren, by the mercies of God, that ye present your bodies a living sacrifice, holy, acceptable unto God, which is your reasonable service.

And be not conformed to this world: but be ye transformed by the renewing of your mind, that ye may prove what is that good, and acceptable, and perfect, will of God."

Romans 12:1-2

Ask yourself this question: Do I know the will of God for my life? There is a difference between the plan of God and the will of God. The plan of God is the *what*. The will of God is the *how*, the desire, means, permission, and limitation of God.

Many people who know what God wants them to do, be, or say, don't know *how* they are going to bring it to pass. I hear them say, "I know what God wants me to do, but I don't know *how* I should go about it." Many have voiced that they know what God wants them to be, but have no idea *how* to become this. Some know what God told them to say, but don't know *how* to get into pulpits or

5

positions to say it. This absence of God's will in people's lives has caused many to be frustrated and bewildered, even to the degree that many who are called quit.

The good, acceptable, and perfect will of God is the most fruitful place for believers to be. When you are in the will of God, you are pleasing to Him. It is good for you and good for God. It is acceptable to you and acceptable to God. It is perfect for your life and fits perfectly into His plan.

You are either in the will of God or you are not. How can there be an in–between? Some people like to justify their slothfulness or sin by calling it God's second best. NO! It is not God's will *at all* for you to be slothful, lazy, unfaithful, unfruitful, and sinful. You are either in the will of God or you are not. You either have His permission or you don't. God is a yea-and-nay God, not a maybe God or an I'll-think-about-it God. God never says, "I don't know."

The will of God is the *how* of God. People all over the world are trying to accomplish the call or command of the Lord on their lives; yet they are not in the will of God. Why? Because God is interested in more than just the end product. He wants to know *how* you finish your project. There is a very noble saying: It doesn't matter if you win or lose, it's *how* you played the game. God cares *how* you are living, *how* you are spending, *how* you are getting the money you need, *how* you are dealing with people, and *how* you are going about accomplishing your goals.

In Christianity, getting the job done is not enough. It is very important *how* you did it. Did you cheat, lie, coerce, manipulate, steal, exaggerate, etc.? You see, getting the plan for your life is very important, but *how* you live and accomplish that plan is just as important.

Remember when you were first born again? When you were with other Christians in church service, you felt sure of your salvation, but when you were all alone, it was so easy to doubt and wonder. But as you worked out your salvation on a daily basis, you were more and more and more sure that you were born again and that God loved you. So is it with the guidance of the Lord. When the Lord is guiding you on a steady basis, you don't need a big word from God. All you need is a little line, a little precept, or a little bit here and a little bit there to add to what you already have. It's like a ship when it is dead in the water. It takes a lot of tugboats to get that massive thing moving in order to steer it properly. Once it is moving, it is much easier to maneuver. When it is cruising along, it only takes a little turn of those rudders, and the vessel will make a big circle in the water. All it takes is a little adjustment because of the momentum.

This is like the will of God for our lives. Don't sit around like a frog on a log until a snake comes along and then jump. Some Christians will jump when there is a thunderstorm, when something is going to eat us up, or when there is a heavy wave about to destroy us. We need to respond to God on a daily basis—even when there are no crises in our lives. I don't know why it's so hard for people to understand this. They won't come to church steadily, they won't pay tithes and give offerings steadily, they won't read the Bible and pray steadily, yet they wonder why they don't know *how* to accomplish the things of God in their lives.

Paul gave us the secret in Romans 12:1-2, which I quoted earlier. *It is a daily, reasonable service for every*

Christian everywhere to present themselves to God every day. This is not a big deal—it's our reasonable service. You're not going to know or partake in the big things of God until you know and partake in your reasonable service.

Renew your mind! This is how you know and prove the will of God. Renew your mind! Stop being so easily persuaded by the systems and practices of the world. Renew your mind.

Isaiah told us the way to show the will of God for our lives. He said it was for those who were weaned from the milk and drawn from the breasts, not babies—but mature believers—those who break away from the world and go after the things of God. Let me quote the scripture here for you:

> *"Whom shall he teach knowledge? and whom shall he make to understand doctrine? them that are weaned from the milk, and drawn from the breasts."*

Isaiah 28:9

So many Christians do their own thing and follow after their own plan. They seem to be too busy (consumed) with the daily routine and demands of the world to dedicate all to God. These same overburdened, weary, sports-fanatic, hobby-infested believers are sooner or later going to have disasters in their lives. Do you know what they will do? They will run to God in despair and horror, and they will want Him to give them the will of God. They will want deliverance and leadership and guidance. They will say that they want to serve God and be obedient if only they knew *how*.

Listen to me, believers. You know the will of God for your life by daily Christian servanthood and disciplines:

"Line upon line, precept upon precept, here a little, there a little." That's right! You accumulate the knowledge and wisdom of God. Each day in Bible study, prayer, and church service you learn a little more about *how* to survive today. That's right!—accumulation, servanthood, presenting yourself daily (not just when you are in a pinch).

> *"Whom shall he teach knowledge? and whom shall he make to understand doctrine? them that are weaned from the milk, and drawn from the breasts."*
>
> Isaiah 28:9

We can know the will of God for our lives by serving Him daily. We can find out *how* to get our things done and *how* to be obedient and *how* to be *what* He wants us to be if we do it consistently as a lifestyle and not sporadically.

It's not enough to know the overall *plan* of God for our lives. We must stay and perform within the boundaries of His will in order to be pleasing to Him.

CHAPTER 3
DO YOU KNOW
THE TIMING OF GOD?
THE *WHEN*

"Cast not away therefore your confidence, which hath great recompence of reward.

For ye have need of patience, that, after ye have done the will of God, ye might receive the promise."

Hebrews 10:35-36

"For the vision is yet for an appointed time, but at the end it shall speak, and not lie: though it tarry, wait for it; because it will surely come, it will not tarry."

Habakkuk 2:3

"To every thing there is a season, and a time to every purpose under the heaven . . ."

Ecclesiastes 3:1

"He hath made every thing beautiful in his time . . ."

Ecclesiastes 3:11

Ask yourself these questions: Do I have the timing of God? Do I know *when* God wants each phase to happen? Once you know the plan of God for your life and ministry and you know the will of God for the plan, then you must find out *when* to put this into effect—"When do I start?"

The *timing* of the Lord doesn't always mean right now. God could say He wants you to do something two or three years from now. You know, God speaks to me sometimes, and He gives me a word for someone. I see that word so clearly that I could write it. God tells me that He will show me who that word is for. In my journeys, when I see this face, I will call it out and give them this word of knowledge. Their hearts will melt before God, and it will help them in their life. There are many times I have been on foreign ground or in other churches preaching, when all of a sudden I will look out, see that face, and it will remind me of days (and sometimes weeks) ago when the Lord instructed me to minister to this particular person.

If we're not careful, we'll want to speak the very moment we receive from God. It's a word in season that really counts, not just a word. (Read Isaiah 50:4.)

We quoted Hebrews, chapter 10, which instructs us to hold on to our confidence and not give it up because it has great recompence of reward. It says that we have need of patience. Patience, patience, patience, patience, that after we have done the will of God, we might receive the promise.

When I went to Bible school, I heard all the teaching about the coming of the Lord and that the end times were here. They told us it was the last of the last days, and there was barely enough time to get out of Bible school. Man, that ate me up. I began to think, There is not enough time to study, I have to go! There isn't enough time, surely there has to be something I can do right now. That stuff consumed me. That is the way some Christians are right now.

They are consumed with their anxiety. They say, I have to do something. I've got to follow my calling. I have been sitting around here too long. Listen, believers, relax and be patient that even after you have done the will of God you might receive the promise. Don't get itchy. Relax and let the Lord work in you.

Crawl as long as you can crawl because there is coming a day that you won't be able to crawl anymore. You'll jump on your feet and you'll start walking and the Father won't let you crawl anymore. He'll say, "No, no. That was the last phase of life, now you get up and walk." We deal with our children this way. We say, "You don't have to crawl anymore, you get up and walk. I'll put your shoes on you, and you had better start walking." Once you begin walking, you have to keep on walking. Walk, walk, walk, walk! Walk as long as you can walk, because when you start running, there is no more walking. You are going to run with this gospel until you cross the finish line. Don't run until you have to run. Just rest in faith. When God wants you to run, He'll tell you.

Have you ever watched a small toddler who is just beginning to walk? As they stagger across the living room floor, they spot something they want from the fancy glass table ahead of them. They get a little urge, and they decide to speed up a little bit. They wobble and fall and crash into things. That is the way a lot of us are. There are a lot of believers who are wobbling and crashing into things because they're pushing the timing or phase of their walk with God.

Don't be disappointed with the particular phase you are in. Enjoy it, the new phase is coming. Just because you are crawling does not mean that you are worthless. Just because you are walking does not mean you are getting nothing done. Don't get in a hurry. Once you start running, you speed up the time that will elapse between you and the end of your vision. You might run for one, twenty, or even eighty years. Whatever the will of the Lord is for you, whatever the plan of God is for you, take time to develop it as you look unto Jesus, the Author and Finisher of your faith.

Now there are other Christians who are too late. They are behind, and they need to catch up. Maybe they have been procrastinating or slothful in their discipleship or work. Some have been fearful to stretch out and go.

God has a perfect moment for you. You may not know it yet, but He does. He makes everything beautiful in His time.

Seek out the Lord and be ready in season and out of season. The divine command to begin doesn't always come when we want it or even when we expect it. God is in charge!

CHAPTER 4
DO YOU WAR ACCORDING
TO PROPHECY?

*"This charge I commit unto thee, son Timothy,
according to the prophecies which went before on
thee, that thou by them mightest war a good warfare . . ."*

1 Timothy 1:18

We are not led by a prophet but by the Spirit of God.
Yet we know there are valid prophetic ministries in the
Kingdom today. Almost everyone enjoys ministry and
prophetic utterance when it is accurate and correct. Many
people, however, would rather have a prophet guide them
than God. Why? Because they are lazy, dull of hearing, or
too busy with the worldly things to seek God's face. No
true prophet of God wishes to take the place of the Holy
Spirit in the lives of believers.

Prophecy is simply a road map given to us from God
to help us find the way. It brings clarity and description to
our path. We should already know our destination. The
road map (prophecy) simply helps us know we are on
course or shows us the best route to take. What a blessing!

You don't get in the car and break out the map and

say, "Let's see, where do we want to go today?" No, you know your destination, you use the map to discover the cleanest, fastest, and safest way to arrive there.

We can war our warfare with these prophetic words. I personally record mine or write them so I can look them over and follow the content. I have received some life-saving words. Even so, we must remember that these are aids to our walk. They are not meant to replace the inner divine leadership or voice of Jesus.

I know people who think they are the mapmakers. They are always prophesying something to someone, and it is evident that it's not God. They tell others they are called to this or that and put divine commission on people. Only Jesus or church leadership can place these authorities on people, not "backdoor" prophets or prophetesses who give direction and callings with no leadership present to judge. (Read 1 Corinthians 14:29-33.)

Many so-called intercessors have been caught up in this. They feel like they should be great receivers instead of prayer warriors. Of course, some preachers hire these people to pray in their stead. Many preachers have these intercessors seeking God on their behalf. This is wrong! Every believer, especially Christian leaders, should seek God on their own. No one should be sent on our behalf to see what God says for us.

Listen, it is not wrong for people to intercede or to pray full-time. The error is made when they pray *instead of* the preacher. There is nothing wrong with praying *with* the preacher.

It almost seems like there is a six–fold ministry gift. You know: apostle, prophet, evangelist, pastor, teacher, and *intercessor*. Of course, the intercessor must be the greatest of these because it is the office that is bringing words from God to rebuke, correct, teach, lead, and inspire the other five gifts. Nonsense! What a shame that we have let it go so far.

To pray means to pray. It is not a department that receives supernatural communication from God to place it upon others. If you do receive, place it upon yourself. Most of these great "receivers" are the people who have weak marriages, poor Christian testimonies, little submission to their leaders, and lack of Christian disciplines.

Please don't be offended. I'm not addressing those who pray properly. I'm not addressing those preachers who seek God themselves. I'm dealing with those who believe that people functioning in these spooky, goofy, fantasizing realms are so spiritually mature.

Prayer is good. *All of us* should pray without ceasing. Prophecy is good. We should not despise or reject it. God does bring revelation and supernatural direction. We should be sensitive to these.

It is our own personal relationship with the Holy Spirit in prayer that will keep us on track. Please don't coerce or manipulate others into thinking that they are called to practice *your* spiritual disciplines. This will hurt them and you.

Prophecy is a road map. Every so often we seem to get lost, even when we know our final destination. Things all of a sudden don't look familiar. We need to look at the map and locate ourselves and reset our course. This is good. Praise God for it! Just be sure that you know the credibility of those who are prophesying to you and that you use the prophecy properly.

> *"Be not deceived: evil communications corrupt good manners."*
>
> 1 Corinthians 15:33

> *"Rejoice evermore.*
>
> *Pray without ceasing.*
>
> *In every thing give thanks: for this is the will of God in Christ Jesus concerning you.*
>
> *Quench not the Spirit.*
>
> *Despise not prophesyings.*
>
> *Prove all things; hold fast that which is good.*
>
> *Abstain from all appearance of evil."*
>
> 1 Thessalonians 5:16-22

CHAPTER 5
DO YOU SEEK CONFIRMATIONS?

"This is the third time I am coming to you. In the mouth of two or three witnesses shall every word be established.

I told you before, and fortell you, as if I were present, the second time; and being absent now I write to them which heretofore have sinned . . ."

2 Corinthians 13:1-2

First of all, don't sit around and wait for confirmation if you don't need it. Many people who know God Himself has given them instructions still sit around and wait for some sign, wonder, or special word to confirm it. Many think every word must be confirmed three times before they can act on it.

Now, confirmation is good. It is very gracious of God to be long-suffering toward us and convince us that what He said is true. Sometimes we get our avenues of communication clogged up. We need to be sure that what we hear is God. In this case, one should wait for confirmation.

When someone says, "The Lord told me to do this, and I'm ready; I'm just waiting for confirmation," they really mean they are procrastinating. When you *know* God told you to do something, get up and get it done. Confirmation is meant to stabilize you when you don't know for sure what God is telling you to do.

People who know they have heard from God do not "fleece" Him, test Him, or sit and wait on Him to give a second or third command. People who hear sharply get it right the first time. They are totally convinced it's God, so they act on it. If they get confirmation, it will catch up with them as they are obedient *to do* what God is saying. If we miss God, He will give a second and third command to us, but this is when we somehow did not respond to the first command.

People who are dull of hearing or in spiritual trouble are usually looking for some extreme display of communication from God. Let me illustrate (1 Kings 19:1-13).

When the great prophet Elijah was in deep spiritual trouble, he prayed he might die. He went from running for his life to sitting under a juniper tree to sitting in the dark, damp dungeon of a cave. There he tried to find God and sort things out in his head. Finally, God began to speak to him and remind him of who and what "Elijah" was. Now remember, this is the great prophet who did so many miracles and heard so often and so accurately the voice of the Lord. Now he is in a cave, and God is trying to get through to him.

The Bible says there was a mighty wind that crumbled the mountains, but as Elijah searched for God (confirmation), He was not found in the wind. Then there was a terrible earthquake, but as Elijah searched for God in the mighty wonder, He wasn't to be found. After all of this, there appeared a fire. Wow—fire! Surely this was confirmation. Surely this was the sign he was looking for, but after he searched for God in the fire, Elijah found He wasn't there. And then . . . and then . . . and then . . . a still small voice spoke to him. This was God!

Are you "fleecing" God or waiting on some super-duper sign from Heaven before you can obey? Shame on you! Listen to that still small voice and get up. Get busy for God.

Look at what Paul wrote. He told the Corinthian church about confirmations. He said that in the mouth of two or three witnesses every word shall be established. (Read 2 Corinthians 13:1.)

Some people think this means three different vessels, but it says three witnesses. Three witnesses do not neces-sarily come from three different people. Now it could be from three different people, but it also could be one person. That's right! It could be your pastor warning you about something once, twice, and yes, even three times. This would be three witnesses of the same word. Look a little closer to what Paul wrote. He said (paraphrased), "I came to you once already [the first witness], and I foretell you as if I were present the second time [the second witness], and being absent, I now write you [the third witness]." Can you see it? Paul was all three witnesses to this particular word. I am a pastor, and I have learned that a pastor many times has to tell certain people certain things at least three times before it sinks in.

I would rather receive confirmation from solid church leadership on three different occasions than from someone I don't even know. If my pastor or leaders in the Lord (who I know are credible) feel so impressed to come to me on three occasions about the same matter, I think I would listen and take it to heart.

Some people don't seem to care who gives them confirmation. I've seen people receive confirmation from the store clerk after she lays down her cigarette and finishes fussing with the last customer. I want more credible ministry than this in my life. If I need confirmation about something, I need to hear from credible vessels. If I need confirmation, it's because I'm not sure of what God is saying to me. I can't afford (and neither can you) to let satan slip in with one of his tricks.

Remember, if you need confirmation, you should wait for it. But if you know for a fact that God has instructed or guided you, go for it. The confirmation will be there when you act on His Word.

> *"And they went forth, and preached every where, the Lord working with them, and confirming the word with signs following. Amen."*
>
> Mark 16:20

When are you seeking confirmation—when you first receive the word (for your sake) or after you've fulfilled the word (for others)?

CHAPTER 6
DO YOU HAVE CHURCH
LEADERSHIP APPROVAL?

"Obey them that have the rule over you, and submit yourselves: for they watch for your souls, as they that must give account, that they may do it with joy, and not with grief: for that is unprofitable for you."

Hebrews 13:17

Ask yourself this question: Do I have the approval of my church leaders to do what I'm about to do?

Many people won't like this section of the book. They will yell out things like, "discipleship error" or "shepherding error" or "spirit of control." I'm telling you, if you are submitting yourself to spiritually-mature leaders (shame on you if you aren't), then you can lean on them when you need them. Your pastor will hear from God and help you to do what God says. If he doesn't feel good about it . . . don't be a brat! You listen to your pastor.

Some people say that their pastor doesn't hear from God, he isn't Spirit-filled, or he won't even consider the things they want to do. Well first of all, blame yourself for committing to a church that doesn't follow the full gospel. It was your own ignorance to submit to men who don't follow the leadership of the Holy Spirit. You should know better! Why were you playing games with your life in the first place?

If my leaders didn't feel good about what I was doing, I would immediately seek God and thoroughly examine my motives, as well as my entire project or leading.

All through the Bible, from Joshua to John the Revelator, we see the supreme role of leadership in the lives of upcoming ministries. Cut your pastor's throat (or anybody's throat for that matter), and you've cut your own throat. It's as simple as that! God will not honor you when you do things dishonorably.

Remember now the content of this book, that the entire purpose was to check your leadings. If God is leading you, your church leaders should hear from God also. (Read Acts 13:1-4.)

I have had several people from the church I pastor leave our work without my approval. Some took time to sit down with me and explain to me (their pastor) what they felt led to do. Others just slyly slipped away, lying and deceiving, following after some feeling, desire, or fantasy. The people who want to follow after God will check and double-check their leadings every step of the way to be sure they are on course with Him.

The problem? Many people are led by their ambition, anger, hurts, feelings, desires, appetites, pride, etc. These people never take time to check their leadings. They are afraid to find out the truth. They are ashamed to face the facts in case the facts differ from their desire. How sad! People would rather follow their desire whether or not it is God's desire for their lives.

Are you itchy and anxious? Are you impatient and short of temperance? Are you following your own plan or pushing your way into something that's not yours? Shame on you!

God has given you spiritual leadership to guard you, feed you, and help lead you. Don't be childish and stupid. Submit to these leaders whom God has given the rule over you. No one is exempt from this. No one gets too big for their britches that they shouldn't listen to leaders. (Read 1 Peter 5:1-6.)

Lower your pride; submit your plans and goals to your pastor. Pray God will use him as an asset to your life. Pray that God will reveal to him the confirmation you need for your life. Pray that God will show him when you are wrong or off course, and pray that he will have the boldness to speak up.

If you really want to stay in God's ways, you will be soft and humble. You will take counsel and seek guidance.

> *"And Jehoash did that which was right in the sight of the Lord all his days wherein Jehoiada the priest instructed him."*
>
> 2 Kings 12:2

So is it with you! As long as you have a priest or pastor to instruct you, you will do that which is right in the sight of the Lord. When you become a know-it-all or a loner, you will begin to stray away a little at a time, and you won't notice it at first.

Believe me—it's worth it to stay humble and listen to leadership. God will guide you in your heart and confirm it in the hearts of your leaders, and you will feel good and clean about your leadings.

PRAYER OF SALVATION

YOU CAN BE SAVED FROM ETERNAL DAMNATION and get God's help now in this life. All you have to do is humble your heart, believe in Christ's work at Calvary for you, and pray the prayer below.

Dear Heavenly Father,

I know that I have sinned and fallen short of Your expectations of me. I have come to realize that I cannot run my own life. I do not want to continue the way I've been living, neither do I want to face an eternity of torment and damnation.

I know that the wages of sin is death, but I can be spared from this through the gift of the Lord Jesus Christ. I believe that He died for me, and I receive His provision now. I will not be ashamed of Him, and I will tell all my friends and family members that I have made this wonderful decision.

Dear Lord Jesus,

Come into my heart now and live in me and be my Savior, Master, and Lord. I will do my very best to chase after You and to learn Your ways by submitting to a pastor, reading my Bible, going to a church that preaches about You, and keeping sin out of my life.

I also ask You to give me the power to be healed from any sickness and disease and to deliver me from those things that have me bound.

I love You and thank You for having me, and I am eagerly looking forward to a long, beautiful relationship with You.

Books by Mark T. Barclay

Beware of Seducing Spirits
This is not a book on demonology. It is a book about the misbehavior of men and women and the seducing and deceiving spirits that influence them to do what they do. Brother Barclay exposes the most prominent seducing spirits of the last days.

Beware of the Sin of Familiarity
This book is a scriptural study on the most devastating sin in the Body of Christ today. The truths in this book will make you aware of this excess familiarity and reveal to you some counterattacks.

Building a Supernatural Church
A guide to pioneering, organizing, and establishing a new local church. This is a fast-reading, simple, instructional guide to leaders and helps people who are working together to build the Church.

Charging the Year 2000
This book will remind you of the last-days' promises of God as well as alert you to the many snares and falsehoods with which satan will try to deceive and seduce last-days' believers. "A handbook for living in the '90s."

Enduring Hardness
God has called His Church an army and the believers soldiers. It is mandatory that all Christians endure hardness as good soldiers of Jesus Christ. This book will help build more backbone in you.

How to Avoid Shipwreck
A book of preventive medicine, helping people stay strong and full of faith. You will be strengthened by this book as you learn how to anchor your soul.

How to Relate to Your Pastor
It is very important in these last days that God's people understand the office of pastor. As we put into practice these principles, the Church will grow in numbers and also increase its vision for the world.

How to Always Reap a Harvest
In this book Brother Barclay explains the principles that make believers successful and fruitful. It shows you how to live a better life and become far more productive and enjoy a full harvest.

Improving Your Performance
Every Christian everywhere needs to read this book. Even leaders will be challenged by this writing. It will help tremendously in the organization and unity of your ministry and working force.

The Making of a Man of God
In this book you'll find some of the greatest, yet simplest, insights to becoming a man or woman of God and to launching your ministry with accuracy and credibility. The longevity of your ministry will be enhanced by the truths herein. You will learn the difference between being a convert, an epistle, a disciple, and a minister.

Preachers of Righteousness

This is not a book for pulpiteers or reverends only but for all of us. It reveals the real ministry style of Jesus Christ and the sold-out commitment of His followers—the most powerful, awesome force on the face of the earth.

The Real Truth About Tithing

This book is a thorough study of God's Word on tithing, which will fully inform believers how to tithe biblically and accurately. You will be armed with the truth, and your life will never be the same!

The Remnant Church

God has always had a people and will always have a people. Brother Barclay speaks of the upcoming revival and how we can be those who are alive and remain when our Master returns.

Sheep, Goats, Wolves

A scriptural yet practical explanation of human behavior in our local churches and how church leaders and members can deal with each other. You will especially enjoy the tests that are in the back of this book.

Six Ways to Check Your Leadings

It seems that staying in the main flow of Jesus is one of the most difficult things for believers to do, and I'm including some preachers. Many people border on mysticism and a world of fantasy. God is not a goofy god. He doesn't intend for His people to be goofy either. This book reveals the six most valuable New Testament ways to live in accuracy and stay perfectly on course. This book is a must for living in the '90s.

The Sin of Lawlessness

Lawlessness always challenges authority and ultimately is designed to hurt people. This book will convict those who are in lawlessness and warn those who could be future victims. It will help your life and straighten your walk with Him.

Warring Mental Warfare

Every person is made up of body, soul, and spirit and fights battles on each of these three fronts. The war against your soul (made up of your mind, will, and emotions) is real and as lethal as spiritual and natural enemies. This book will help you identify, war against, and defeat the enemies of your soul. Learn to quit coping with depression, anxiety, fear, and other hurts and begin conquering them now!

Basic Christian Handbook (mini book)

This mini book is packed full of scriptures and basic information needed for a solid Christian foundation. It would make an inexpensive and effective tract and is a must for new converts. Many church workers are using it for altar counseling.

The Captain's Mantle (mini book)

Something happened in the cave Adullum. Find out how 400 distressed, indebted, and discontented men came out of that cave as one of the most awesome armies in history.